Informing the legislative debate since 1914 _____

The State of Campaign Finance Policy: Recent Developments and Issues for Congress

R. Sam Garrett

Specialist in American National Government

June 23, 2014

Congressional Research Service

7-5700

www.crs.gov

R41542

Summary

Major changes have occurred in campaign finance policy since 2002, when Congress substantially amended campaign finance law via the Bipartisan Campaign Reform Act (BCRA). The Supreme Court's 2010 ruling in *Citizens United* and a related lower-court decision, *SpeechNow.org v. FEC*, arguably represent the most fundamental changes to campaign finance law in decades. *Citizens United* lifted a previous ban on corporate (and union) independent expenditures advocating election or defeat of candidates. *SpeechNow* permitted unlimited contributions to such expenditures and facilitated the advent of super PACs. Although campaign finance policy remains the subject of intense debate and public interest, there have been few legislative or regulatory changes to respond to the 2010 court rulings. This report considers these and other developments in campaign finance policy and comments on areas of potential conflict and consensus. In another recent major change, the Supreme Court invalidated aggregate contribution limits in April 2014 (*McCutcheon v. FEC*).

Legislative activity to respond to the rulings has focused on the DISCLOSE Act, which passed the House during the 111th Congress, and was reintroduced during the 112th and 113th Congresses (H.R. 148). Recent alternatives, which include some elements of DISCLOSE, include 113th Congress bills such as Senators Wyden and Murkowski's S. 791, or proposals that would require additional disclosure from certain 501(c) groups.

Two campaign finance bills have become law during the 113th Congress. In December 2013, President Obama signed H.R. 3487. The law extends Federal Election Commission (FEC) authority to conduct the Administrative Fine Program. In April 2014, President Obama signed H.R. 2019, which terminates public financing for presidential nominating conventions. Other bills have been the subject of hearings, markups, or both in the House or Senate. H.R. 94 and H.R. 95 would repeal part or all of the presidential public financing program. H.R. 1994 would repeal the Election Assistance Commission and return some functions to the FEC. S. 375 would require Senate political committees to electronically file campaign finance reports with the FEC. Two appropriations measures contain provisions related to campaign finance. H.R. 2786 would prohibit disclosure of certain political spending as a condition of the government-contracting process. S. 1371 would require electronic filing of Senate campaign finance reports. S.J.Res. 19 proposes a constitutional amendment permitting additional regulation of campaign-related money. A hearing is scheduled on H.R. 186, which would permit candidates to designate someone other than the campaign treasurer to disburse funds if the candidate died.

Debate has also continued at federal agencies and in the courts. Debate in Congress and elsewhere has continued over the FEC's enforcement practices. Amid apparent stalemate at the FEC, some observers have called for an increased role for federal agencies, such as the Federal Communications Commission, Internal Revenue Service, or Securities and Exchange Commission in policy areas related to campaign finance policy—a topic that remains controversial. In addition, on September 23, 2013, the Senate confirmed two nominees to the Federal Election Commission.

This version of the report includes updated material that emphasizes the issues most prominently before the 113th Congress. It also discusses foundational information about major elements of campaign finance policy. Some issues discussed in previous versions of the report, which appear to be less timely than they were in the past, have been excluded from this version. This report will be updated occasionally to reflect major developments.

Contents

Tables

Contacts

Introduction

Federal law has regulated money in elections for more than a century.[1] Concerns about limiting the potential for corruption and informing voters have been at the heart of that law and related regulations and judicial decisions. Restrictions on private money in campaigns, particularly large contributions, have been a common theme throughout the history of federal campaign finance law. The roles of corporations, unions, interest groups, and private funding from individuals have attracted consistent regulatory attention. Congress has also required that certain information about campaigns' financial transactions be made public. Collectively, three principles embodied in this regulatory tradition—limits on sources of funds, limits on contributions, and disclosure of information about these funds—constitute ongoing themes in federal campaign finance policy.

Throughout most of the 20th century, campaign finance policy was marked by broad legislation enacted sporadically. Major legislative action on campaign finance issues remains rare. Since the 1990s, however, momentum on federal campaign finance policy, including regulatory and judicial action, has arguably increased. Congress last enacted major campaign finance legislation in 2002. The Bipartisan Campaign Reform Act (BCRA) largely banned unregulated *soft money*[2] in federal elections and restricted funding sources for pre-election broadcast advertising known as *electioneering communications*. As BCRA was implemented, regulatory developments at the Federal Election Commission (FEC), and some court cases, stirred controversy and renewed popular and congressional attention to campaign finance issues. Since BCRA, Congress has also continued to explore legislative options and has made comparatively minor amendments to the nation's campaign finance law.

Some of the most recent notable campaign finance developments have occurred at the Supreme Court. On April 2, 2014, the Court invalidated aggregate contribution limits in *McCutcheon v.*

---

[1] The 1907 Tillman Act (34 Stat. 864), which prohibited federal contributions from nationally chartered banks and corporations, is generally regarded as the first major federal campaign finance law. The 1925 Federal Corrupt Practices Act (43 Stat. 1070) was arguably the first federal statute combining multiple campaign finance provisions, particularly disclosure requirements first enacted in 1910 and 1911 (36 Stat. 822 and 37 Stat. 25). An 1867 statute barred requiring political contributions from naval yard workers (14 Stat. 489 (March 2, 1867)). This appears to be the first federal law concerning campaign finance. The Pendleton Act (22 Stat. 403), which created the civil service system is also sometimes cited as an early campaign finance measure because it banned receiving a public office in exchange for a political contributions (see 22 Stat. 404). For additional historical discussion of the evolution of campaign finance law and policy, see Anthony Corrado et al., *The New Campaign Finance Sourcebook* (Washington, DC: Brookings Institution Press, 2005), pp. 7-47. See also, for example, Kurt Hohenstein, *Coining Corruption: The Making of the American Campaign Finance System* (DeKalb, IL: Northern Illinois University Press, 2007), Robert E. Mutch, *Campaigns, Congress, and Courts: The Making of Federal Campaign Finance Law* (New York: Praeger, 1988), Raymond J. La Raja, *Small Change: Money, Political Parties, and Campaign Finance Reform* (Ann Arbor, MI: University of Michigan Press, 2008), pp. 43-80, and *Money and PoliticS*, ed. Paula Baker (University Park, PA: The Pennsylvania State University Press, 2002).

[2] *Soft money* is a term of art referring to funds generally believed to influence federal elections but not regulated under federal election law. Soft money stands in contrast to *hard money*. The latter is a term of art referring to funds that are generally subject to regulation under federal election law, such as restrictions on funding sources and contribution amounts. These terms are not defined in federal election law. For an overview, see, for example, David B. Magleby, "Outside Money in the 2002 Congressional Elections," in *The Last Hurrah? Soft Money and Issue Advocacy in the 2002 Congressional Elections*, ed. David B. Magleby and J. Quin Monson (Washington: Brookings Institution Press, 2004), pp. 10-13.

FEC. "Base" limits capping the amounts that donors may give to individual candidates still apply.[3]

An arguably more consequential ruling occurred four years earlier in *Citizens United v. Federal Election Commission*.[4] In its highly anticipated January 21, 2010, *Citizens United* ruling, the Court lifted the long-standing Federal Election Campaign Act (FECA) prohibition on corporations—and, implicitly, unions—using their general treasury funds for political advertisements known as *independent expenditures* and *electioneering communications*. *Independent expenditures* explicitly call for election or defeat of political candidates (known as *express advocacy*), may occur at any time, and are usually (but not always) broadcast advertisements. They must also be uncoordinated with the campaign in question.[5] *Electioneering communications* are defined only as broadcast advertising, are aired during specific pre-election windows, and might discuss a candidate, but do not explicitly call for election or defeat (known as *issue advocacy*).[6] Additional discussion appears later in this report.

The *Citizens United* ruling spurred substantial legislative action during the 111th Congress and continued interest during the 112th and 113th Congresses.[7] The ruling was, however, only the latest—albeit perhaps the most monumental—shift in federal campaign finance policy to occur in recent years. In another 2010 decision, *SpeechNow.org v. Federal Election Commission*, the U.S. Court of Appeals for the District of Columbia held that contributions to political action committees (PACs) that make only independent expenditures cannot be limited—a development that led to formation of "super PACs."[8] Campaigns, parties, and other groups must adapt to these new realities, just as Congress and federal agencies must decide how or whether to respond. In addition, Congress, courts, the FEC, and other administrative agencies continue to examine various other campaign finance policy matters.

As Congress considers how to proceed, it may be appropriate to take stock of the current landscape and to examine what has changed, what has not, and which policy issues and options might be relevant. This report provides a resource for that discussion. It includes an overview of selected recent events in campaign finance policy and comments on how those events might affect future policy considerations. The most prominent issues are directly related to *Citizens United* and *SpeechNow*. Others, such as public financing and FEC matters, would be timely regardless of recent litigation. Historical themes of limiting potential corruption and promoting

---

[3] For additional policy discussion, as well as citations to other CRS products that cover legal issues, see CRS Report R43334, *Campaign Contribution Limits: Selected Questions About McCutcheon and Policy Issues for Congress*, by R. Sam Garrett.

[4] 130 S. Ct. 876 (2010). For legal analyses of the case, see CRS Report R41045, *The Constitutionality of Regulating Corporate Expenditures: A Brief Analysis of the Supreme Court Ruling in Citizens United v. FEC*, by L. Paige Whitaker; and CRS Report R41096, *Legislative Options After Citizens United v. FEC: Constitutional and Legal Issues*, by L. Paige Whitaker et al.

[5] On the definition of *independent expenditures*, see 2 U.S.C. 431 §17.

[6] On the definition of *electioneering communications*, see 2 U.S.C. 434 §(f)(3).

[7] For additional discussion of activity during the 111th Congress, see CRS Report R41054, *Campaign Finance Policy After Citizens United v. Federal Election Commission: Issues and Options for Congress*, by R. Sam Garrett; and CRS Report R41264, *The DISCLOSE Act: Overview and Analysis*, by R. Sam Garrett, L. Paige Whitaker, and Erika K. Lunder.

[8] For additional discussion of *SpeechNow*, see CRS Report RS22895, *527 Groups and Campaign Activity: Analysis Under Campaign Finance and Tax Laws*, by L. Paige Whitaker and Erika K. Lunder. On super PACs, see CRS Report R42042, *Super PACs in Federal Elections: Overview and Issues for Congress*, by R. Sam Garrett.

transparency underlie the debate on each of these issues and on campaign finance policy as a whole.

Before proceeding, explaining the report's boundaries may help readers. This report is intended to provide an accessible overview of major policy issues facing Congress. Citations to other CRS products, which provide additional information, appear where relevant. The report discusses selected litigation to demonstrate how those events have changed the campaign finance landscape and affected the policy issues that may confront Congress, but it is not a constitutional or legal analysis. Finally, this version of the report contains both additions of new material and deletions of old material compared with previous versions. This update emphasizes those topics that appear to be most relevant for the 113th Congress, while also providing historical background that is more broadly applicable.

Development of Modern Campaign Finance Law

Policy Background

Dozens or hundreds of campaign finance bills have been introduced in each Congress since the 1970s. In fact, more than 1,000 campaign finance measures have been introduced since the 93rd Congress (1973-1974).[9] Nonetheless, major changes in campaign finance law have been rare. A generation passed between FECA and BCRA, the two most prominent campaign finance statutes of the past 50 years. Federal courts and the FEC played active roles in interpreting and implementing both statutes and others. The *Citizens United* and *SpeechNow* decisions appear to represent the next chapter in campaign finance policy and are the focus of recent attention in Congress and elsewhere.

Over time and in all facets of the policy process, anti-corruption themes have been consistently evident. Specifically, federal campaign finance law seeks to limit corruption or apparent corruption in the lawmaking process that might result from monetary contributions. Campaign finance law also seeks to inform voters about sources and amounts of contributions. In general, Congress has attempted to limit potential corruption and increase voter information through two major policy approaches:

- limiting sources and amounts of financial contributions and

- requiring disclosure about contributions and expenditures.

Another hallmark of the nation's campaign finance policy concerns spending restrictions. Congress has occasionally placed restrictions on the amount candidates can spend, as it did initially through FECA. Today, as discussed later in this report, candidates and political

---

[9] This figure is a CRS estimate and may understate the total number of relevant bills. This estimate is based on a search of the Legislative Information System (LIS) for bills introduced between the 93rd and 113th Congresses that included the terms "campaign finance" or "Federal Election Campaign Act" in the bill title or summary. The search was limited to measures referred to the Committee on House Administration or Senate Committee on Rules and Administration. Other bills not reflected here may also be relevant, just as some of the bills included here are not principally related to campaign finance. The bills are also not all unique; some include identical legislative language introduced in multiple Congresses and in both chambers.

committees can generally spend unlimited amounts on their campaigns, as long as those funds are not coordinated with other parties or candidates.[10]

The Federal Election Campaign Act (FECA)

Modern campaign finance law was largely shaped in the 1970s, particularly through FECA.[11] First enacted in 1971 and substantially amended in 1974, 1976, and 1979, FECA remains the foundation of the nation's campaign finance law.[12] As originally enacted, FECA subsumed previous campaign finance statutes, such as the 1925 Corrupt Practices Act, which, by the 1970s, were largely regarded as ineffective, antiquated, or both.[13] The 1971 FECA principally mandated reporting requirements similar to those in place today, such as quarterly reporting of a political committee's receipts and expenditures. Subsequent amendments to FECA played a major role in shaping campaign finance policy as it is understood today. In brief:

- Among other requirements, the 1974 amendments, enacted in response to the Watergate scandal, placed contribution and spending limits on campaigns. The 1974 amendments also established the FEC.

- After the 1974 amendments were enacted, the first in a series of prominent legal challenges (most of which are beyond the scope of this report) came before the Supreme Court of the United States.[14] In its landmark *Buckley v. Valeo* (1976) ruling, the Court declared mandatory spending limits unconstitutional (except for publicly financed presidential candidates) and invalidated the original appointment structure for the FEC.

- Congress responded to *Buckley* through the 1976 FECA amendments, which reconstituted the FEC, established new contribution limits, and addressed various PAC and presidential public financing issues.

- The 1979 amendments simplified reporting requirements for some political committees and individuals.

To summarize, the 1970s were devoted primarily to establishing and testing limits on contributions and expenditures, creating a disclosure regime, and constructing the FEC to administer the nation's campaign finance laws.

Despite minor amendments, FECA remained essentially uninterrupted for the next 20 years. Although there were relatively narrow legislative changes of FECA and other statutes, such as the

---

[10] *Political committees* include candidate committees, party committees, and PACs. See 2 U.S.C. §431(4).

[11] FECA is 2 U.S.C. §431 *et seq*. Congress first addressed modern campaign finance issues in the 1970s through the 1971 Revenue Act, which established the presidential public financing program. The 1970s are primarily remembered, however, for enactment of and amendments to FECA. For additional discussion of presidential public financing, including an initial 1960s public financing program that was quickly repealed, see CRS Report RL34534, *Public Financing of Presidential Campaigns: Overview and Analysis*, by R. Sam Garrett.

[12] On the 1971 FECA, see P.L. 92-225. On the 1974, 1976, and 1979 amendments, see P.L. 93-443, P.L. 94-283, and P.L. 96-187 respectively.

[13] The Corrupt Practices Act, which FECA generally supersedes, is 43 Stat. 1070.

[14] For additional discussion, see CRS Report RL30669, *The Constitutionality of Campaign Finance Regulation: Buckley v. Valeo and Its Supreme Court Progeny*, by L. Paige Whitaker.

1986 repeal[15] of tax credits for political contributions, much of the debate during the 1980s and early 1990s focused on the role of interest groups, especially PACs.[16]

The Bipartisan Campaign Reform Act (BCRA) and Beyond

By the 1990s, attention began to shift to perceived loopholes in FECA. Two issues—soft money and issue advocacy (issue advertising)—were especially prominent. *Soft money* is a term of art referring to funds generally perceived to influence elections but not regulated by campaign finance law. At the federal level before BCRA, soft money came principally in the form of large contributions from otherwise prohibited sources, and went to party committees for "party-building" activities that indirectly supported elections. Similarly, *issue advocacy* traditionally fell outside FECA regulation because these advertisements praised or criticized a federal candidate— often by urging voters to contact the candidate—but did not explicitly call for election or defeat of the candidate (which would be *express advocacy*).

In response to these and other concerns, BCRA specified several reforms.[17] Among other provisions, the act banned national parties, federal candidates, and officeholders from raising soft money in federal elections; increased most contribution limits; and placed additional restrictions on pre-election issue advocacy. Specifically, the act's *electioneering communications* provision prohibited corporations and unions from using their treasury funds to air broadcast ads referring to clearly identified federal candidates within 60 days of a general election or 30 days of a primary election or caucus.

After Congress enacted BCRA, momentum on federal campaign finance policy issues arguably shifted to the FEC and the courts. Implementing and interpreting BCRA were especially prominent issues. Noteworthy post-BCRA events include the following:

- The Supreme Court upheld most of BCRA's provisions in a 2003 facial challenge (*McConnell v. Federal Election Commission*).[18]

- Over time, the Court held aspects of BCRA unconstitutional as applied to specific circumstances. These included a 2008 ruling related to additional fundraising permitted for congressional candidates facing self-financed opponents (the "Millionaire's Amendment," *Davis v. Federal Election Commission*) and a 2007 ruling on the electioneering communication provision's restrictions on advertising by a 501(c)(4) advocacy organization (*Wisconsin Right to Life v. Federal Election Commission*).[19]

---

[15] See P.L. 99-514 §112. Congress repealed a tax deduction for political contributions in 1978. See P.L. 95-600 §113.

[16] See, for example, Robert E. Mutch, *Campaigns, Congress, and Courts: The Making of Federal Campaign Finance Law* (New York: Praeger, 1988); and *Risky Business? PAC Decisionmaking in Congressional Elections*, ed. Robert Biersack, Clyde S. Wilcox, and Paul S. Herrnson (Armonk, NY: M.E. Sharpe, 1994).

[17] BCRA is P.L. 107-155; 116 Stat. 81. BCRA amended FECA, which appears at 2 U.S.C. §431 *et seq*. BCRA is also known as *McCain-Feingold*.

[18] For additional discussion, see CRS Report RL32245, *Campaign Finance Law: A Legal Analysis of the Supreme Court Ruling in McConnell v. FEC*, by L. Paige Whitaker; and CRS Report RL30669, *The Constitutionality of Campaign Finance Regulation: Buckley v. Valeo and Its Supreme Court Progeny*, by L. Paige Whitaker.

[19] For additional discussion, see CRS Report RS22920, *Campaign Finance Law and the Constitutionality of the "Millionaire's Amendment": An Analysis of Davis v. Federal Election Commission*, by L. Paige Whitaker; CRS Report RS22687, *The Constitutionality of Regulating Political Advertisements: An Analysis of Federal Election Commission v.* (continued...)

- Since 2002, the FEC has undertaken several rulemakings related to BCRA and other topics. Complicated subject matter, protracted debate among commissioners, and litigation have made some rulemakings lengthy and controversial.[20]

- Congress has also enacted some additional amendments to campaign finance law since BCRA. Most notably, the 2007 Honest Leadership and Open Government Act (HLOGA) placed new disclosure requirements on lobbyists' campaign contributions (certain bundled contributions) and restricted campaign travel aboard private aircraft.[21]

What Has Changed Most Recently and What Has Not?

Congress most recently considered major campaign finance legislation in response to the 2010 *Citizens United* decision. The Senate declined to amend federal campaign finance law in response to the decision, although the DISCLOSE Act passed the House during the 111th Congress (discussed below). Neither chamber passed changes to campaign finance law during the 112th Congress. The 113th Congress has also witnessed relatively little legislative action beyond introduction on campaign finance matters, although how or whether to address the post-*Citizens United* environment continues to be a major area of emphasis among those pursuing legislation, oversight, or both. As noted below, congressional attention to FEC matters and pending litigation also appears to be on the horizon during the 113th Congress.

The FEC has not issued new rules to implement the 2010 *SpeechNow* and *Citizens United* decisions. After disagreement throughout 2011, in December 2011 FEC commissioners approved a notice of proposed rulemaking (NPRM) posing questions about some aspects of what form post-*Citizens United* rules should take.[22] The agency held a hearing on the NPRM in March 2012. A final rulemaking calendar is unclear. Whatever the rulemaking outcome, *Citizens United* makes clear that corporations and unions may now make unlimited IEs supporting or opposing particular candidates and ECs that refer to those candidates during pre-election periods. In addition, in July 2010, the FEC approved two relevant advisory opinions (AOs). Afterward, some corporations and other organizations began making previously prohibited expenditures or raising previously prohibited funds for electioneering communications or independent expenditures. Discussion of other ongoing agency matters appears in the "FEC Issues" section of this report.

Following these developments (especially *Citizens United*), some have suggested that campaign finance policy has been fundamentally altered. As the following discussion shows, some major

---

(...continued)

Wisconsin Right to Life, Inc., by L. Paige Whitaker; and CRS Report RL34324, *Campaign Finance: Legislative Developments and Policy Issues in the 110th Congress*, by R. Sam Garrett.

[20] For example, rulemakings on various BCRA provisions resulted in a series of at least three lawsuits covering six years. These are the *Shays and Meehan v. Federal Election Commission* cases.

[21] For additional discussion, see CRS Report R40091, *Campaign Finance: Potential Legislative and Policy Issues for the 111th Congress*, by R. Sam Garrett. HLOGA is primarily an ethics and lobbying statute. For additional discussion, see, for example, CRS Report R40245, *Lobbying Registration and Disclosure: Before and After the Enactment of the Honest Leadership and Open Government Act of 2007*, by Jacob R. Straus.

[22] Federal Election Commission, "Independent Expenditures and Electioneering Communications by Corporations and Labor Organizations," 248 *Federal Register* 80803, December 27, 2011.

historical provisions have been invalidated. Other hallmarks of campaign finance policy remain unchanged.

What Has Changed

Unlimited Corporate and Union Spending on Independent Expenditures and Electioneering Communications

In January 2010, the Supreme Court issued a 5-4 decision in *Citizens United v. Federal Election Commission*.[23] In brief, the opinion invalidated FECA's prohibitions on corporate and union treasury funding of independent expenditures and electioneering communications.[24] As a consequence of *Citizens United*, corporations and unions are now free to use their treasury funds to air political advertisements explicitly calling for election or defeat of federal or state candidates (independent expenditures) or advertisements that refer to those candidates during pre-election periods, but do not necessarily explicitly call for their election or defeat (electioneering communications). Previously, such advertising would generally have had to be financed through voluntary contributions raised by PACs affiliated with unions or corporations.

In the 111th Congress, the House and Senate considered various legislation designed to increase public availability of information (*disclosure*) about corporate and union spending following *Citizens United*. Most congressional attention responding to the ruling focused on the DISCLOSE Act (H.R. 5175; S. 3295; S. 3628). The House of Representatives passed H.R. 5175, with amendments, on June 24, 2010, by a 219-206 vote. By a 57-41 vote, the Senate declined to invoke cloture on companion bill, S. 3628, on July 27, 2010.[25] A second cloture vote failed (59-39) on September 23, 2010.[26] No additional action on the bill occurred during the 111th Congress.

Three largely similar versions of the DISCLOSE Act were introduced in the 112th Congress. On March 29, 2012, the Senate Committee on Rules and Administration held a hearing on the first-introduced Senate bill, S. 2219 (Whitehouse). On July 10, 2012, Senator Whitehouse introduced a second version of the bill, S. 3369. The Senate debated a motion to proceed to the measure in July 2012 but declined (by a 53-45 vote) to invoke cloture.[27] Representative Van Hollen's House companion version of the DISCLOSE Act, H.R. 4010, was referred to the Committees on House Administration and Judiciary. The bill was not the subject of additional action, although

---

[23] 130 S. Ct. 876 (2010). For additional discussion, see CRS Report R41054, *Campaign Finance Policy After Citizens United v. Federal Election Commission: Issues and Options for Congress*, by R. Sam Garrett; CRS Report R41045, *The Constitutionality of Regulating Corporate Expenditures: A Brief Analysis of the Supreme Court Ruling in Citizens United v. FEC*, by L. Paige Whitaker; CRS Report R41096, *Legislative Options After Citizens United v. FEC: Constitutional and Legal Issues*, by L. Paige Whitaker et al.; and CRS Report R41264, *The DISCLOSE Act: Overview and Analysis*, by R. Sam Garrett, L. Paige Whitaker, and Erika K. Lunder.

[24] As noted elsewhere in this report, BCRA instituted the electioneering communication provision. BCRA amended FECA. See CRS Report RL30669, *The Constitutionality of Campaign Finance Regulation: Buckley v. Valeo and Its Supreme Court Progeny*, by L. Paige Whitaker.

[25] "DISCLOSE Act—Motion to Proceed," Senate vote 220, *Congressional Record*, daily edition, vol. 156 (July 27, 2010), p. S6285.

[26] "DISCLOSE Act—Motion to Proceed—Resumed," Senate vote 240, *Congressional Record*, daily edition, vol. 156 (September 23, 2010), p. S7388.

[27] "DISCLOSE Act—Motion to Proceed—Continued," Rollcall vote 180, *Congressional Record*, daily edition, vol. 158 (July 17, 2012), p. S5072.

Representative Van Hollen filed a discharge petition on the measure.[28] He re-introduced the DISCLOSE Act as H.R. 148 during the 113th Congress.[29] As of this writing, the measure does not have a Senate companion.

Unlimited Contributions to Independent-Expenditure-Only Political Action Committees (Super PACs)

Another notable development concerns contributions to a new category of PACs. In brief, on March 26, 2010, the U.S. Court of Appeals for the District of Columbia held in *SpeechNow.org v. Federal Election Commission*[30] that contributions to PACs that make only independent expenditures—but not contributions—could not be constitutionally limited. As a result, these entities, commonly called *super PACs*, may accept previously prohibited amounts and sources of funds, including large corporate, union, or individual contributions used to advocate for election or defeat of federal candidates. Existing reporting requirements for PACs appear to apply to super PACs, meaning that contributions and expenditures would have to be disclosed to the FEC. Additional discussion of super PACs appears in another CRS product.[31]

Unlimited Contributions to Certain Non-Connected Political Action Committees (PACs)

As the ramifications of *Citizens United* and *SpeechNow* continued to unfold, other forms of unlimited fundraising were also permitted. In October 2011 the FEC announced that, in response to an agreement reached in a case brought after *SpeechNow* (*Carey v. FEC*),[32] the agency would permit *nonconnected* PACs—those that are unaffiliated with corporations or unions—to accept unlimited contributions for use in independent expenditures. The agency directed PACs choosing to do so to keep the independent expenditure contributions in a separate bank account from the one used to make contributions to federal candidates.[33] As such, nonconnected PACs that want to raise unlimited sums for independent expenditures are now able to create a separate bank account and meet additional reporting obligations rather than forming a separate super PAC. Super PACs have, nonetheless, continued to be an important force in American politics because only some traditional PACs would qualify for the *Carey* exemption to fundraising limits.[34] Approximately 50

---

[28] Discharge petitions with signatories are available on the Clerk of the House website. In this case, see petition no. 0004, 112th Cong., 2nd Sess., July 12, 2012, http://clerk house.gov/112/lrc/pd/petitions/DisPet0004 xml.

[29] CRS congressional distribution memoranda providing additional comparison of current and previous versions of the DISCLOSE Act are available to House and Senate requesters from the author of this report. See *Comparison of Selected Versions of the DISCLOSE Act*, by R. Sam Garrett, various dates, CRS congressional distribution memoranda. See also *Comparison of Current Law with Selected Versions of the DISCLOSE Act and the Follow the Money Act*, August 20, 2013, by R. Sam Garrett, Erika Lunder, and L. Paige Whitaker. These memoranda were prepared for distribution to multiple congressional offices.

[30] 599 F.3d 686 (D.C. Cir. 2010).

[31] See CRS Report R42042, *Super PACs in Federal Elections: Overview and Issues for Congress*, by R. Sam Garrett. On their role in presidential elections, see also CRS Report R42139, *Contemporary Developments in Presidential Elections*, by Kevin J. Coleman, R. Sam Garrett, and Thomas H. Neale.

[32] Civ. No. 11-259-RMC (D.D.C. 2011).

[33] Federal Election Commission, "FEC Statement on Carey v. FEC: Reporting Guidance for Political Committees that Maintain a Non-Contribution Account," press release, October 5, 2011, http://www fec.gov/press/Press2011/20111006postcarey.shtml.

[34] In particular, the exemption only applies to nonconnected PACs (i.e., those that exist independently as PACs and are (continued...)

---

nonconnected PACs filed notice with the FEC that they planned to raise unlimited funds during the 2012 election cycle.[35]

Some Funding for Publicly Financed State-Level Candidates

On June 27, 2011, the Supreme Court of the United States issued a 5-4 opinion in the consolidated case *Arizona Free Enterprise Club's Freedom Club PAC et al. v. Bennett* and *McComish v. Bennett*.[36] The decision invalidated portions of Arizona's public financing program for state-level candidates.[37] The majority opinion, authored by Chief Justice Roberts, held that the state's use of matching funds (also called *trigger funds, rescue funds*, or *escape hatch funds*) unconstitutionally burdened privately financed candidates' free speech and did not meet a compelling state interest.[38]

The decision has been most relevant for state-level public financing programs, as a similar matching fund system does not operate at the federal level. It could, however, affect policy options for updating the presidential public financing program or proposals to publicly finance House and Senate campaigns.

U.S. District Court Opinion on Electioneering Communications Disclosure

One of the most controversial elements of campaign finance disclosure concerns identifying donors to organizations that make electioneering communications and independent expenditures.[39] Although FECA requires that those giving more than $200 "for the purpose of furthering" IEs must be identified in political committees' disclosure reports filed with the FEC, the "purpose of furthering" language does not appear in the portion of FECA covering ECs. FEC regulations, however, also use the "purpose of furthering" language as a threshold for identifying donors to corporations or unions making ECs.[40] As a result, some contend that the EC regulations improperly permit those contributing to ECs to avoid disclosure by making unrestricted contributions (i.e., *not* "for the purpose of furthering" ECs).[41] On the basis of that argument and others, Representative Van Hollen sued the FEC in 2011. On March 30, 2012, Judge Amy Berman Jackson, of the U.S. District Court for the District of Columbia, ruled in *Van Hollen v.*

(...continued)

not affiliated with a parent organization, such as an interest group or labor union).

[35] This information is available on the FEC website at http://www.fec.gov/press/press2011/2012PoliticalCommitteeswithNon-ContributionAccounts.shtml.

[36] 131 S.Ct. 2806 (2011). The slip opinion is available at http://www.supremecourt.gov/opinions/10pdf/10-238.pdf.

[37] For additional discussion of state-level public financing, see the "State Experiences with Public Financing" section of CRS Report RL33814, *Public Financing of Congressional Campaigns: Overview and Analysis*, by R. Sam Garrett.

[38] For a discussion of Court treatment of campaign finance issues since *Buckley*, see CRS Report RL30669, *The Constitutionality of Campaign Finance Regulation: Buckley v. Valeo and Its Supreme Court Progeny*, by L. Paige Whitaker.

[39] See, for example, the "Potential Policy Questions and Issues for Consideration" section in CRS Report R42042, *Super PACs in Federal Elections: Overview and Issues for Congress*, by R. Sam Garrett.

[40] 11 C.F.R. §104.20(c)(9).

[41] The same argument is made concerning IE disclosure, although the absence of the "purpose of furthering" language is unique to EC provisions in FECA.

FEC that the agency had exceeded its authority by "narrow[ing] the disclosure requirement [enacted by Congress] through agency rulemaking."[42]

Although a legal analysis of the case is beyond the scope of this report, the decision appeared to require disclosure of the identity of all contributors of at least $1,000 to an entity making ECs, unless the ECs were made from a segregated account, in which case only those contributors who donated at least $1,000 to that account would be disclosed.[43] On July 27, 2012, the FEC announced that, pending resolution of an appeal from defendant-intervenors or issuance of new regulations, those making ECs should report "the name and address of each donor who donated an amount aggregating $1,000 or more to the person making the disbursement, aggregating since the first day of the preceding calendar year."[44] The requirement was retroactive to March 30, 2012, the day of Judge Berman Jackson's ruling. However, on September 18, 2012, the U.S. Court of Appeals for the District of Columbia Circuit reversed the District Court judgment and remanded the case, with instructions to refer the matter back to the FEC. On October 4, 2012, the commission notified the District Court that it would not initiate a rulemaking and would continue to defend the regulation.[45] The case remains pending before the district court.

The potential for additional legal or regulatory action surrounding *Van Hollen* remains unclear. Members of the commission issued competing public statements expressing their disagreement over whether the decision should have been appealed and whether it provides sufficient guidance to those seeking to comply with the law.[46] This development, in addition to other "deadlocked" votes on some controversial, recent matters, suggests that reaching agreement among at least four commissioners—as required by FECA—to amend commission rules to implement the *Van Hollen* ruling could be difficult.[47]

Federal Communications Commission Rules on Political Advertising Disclosure

The Federal Election Commission has primary regulatory responsibility for civil enforcement of campaign finance law. As discussed elsewhere in this report, other agencies also play roles in some aspects of campaign finance regulation. Telecommunications law administered by the Federal Communications Commission (FCC)—a topic that is otherwise beyond the scope of this report—has implications for elements of political advertising transparency.

---

[42] *Van Hollen v. FEC*, 2012 U.S. Dist. LEXIS 44342 (D.D.C. March 30, 2012).

[43] 2 U.S.C. §434(f)(2)(E),(F).

[44] Federal Election Commission, "FEC Statement on *Van Hollen v. FEC*," press release, July 27, 2012, http://www.fec.gov/press/press2012/20120727_VanHollen_v_FEC.shtml.

[45] For a brief overview, see Federal Election Commission, "Van Hollen v. FEC," *Record* newsletter, November 2012, http://www.fec.gov/pages/fecrecord/2012/november/vhvfec.shtml.

[46] See Statement of Vice Chair [Ellen] Weintraub and Commissioner [Cynthia] Bauerly regarding the Commission's decision not to appeal the decision in Van Hollen v. FEC, Federal Election Commission, Washington, DC , April 27, 2012, http://www.fec.gov/members/statements/ELW_CLB_statement_on_VH_appeal.pdf; and Statement on Van Hollen v. FEC. Chair Caroline C. Hunter and Commissioners Donald F. McGahn and Matthew S. Petersen, Federal Election Commission, Washington, DC, n.d., http://www.fec.gov/members/statements/Van_Hollen_statement-Hunter_McGahn_Petersen.pdf.

[47] For an overview of commission voting requirements, see CRS Report RS22780, *The Federal Election Commission (FEC) With Fewer than Four Members: Overview of Policy Implications*, by R. Sam Garrett.

In BCRA, Congress required broadcasters to place information about, among other matters, political advertising prices and purchases in a "political file" available for public inspection.[48] Partially in response to *Citizens United*, in 2011 the FCC revisited rulemaking proceedings the agency began in 2007 to consider whether broadcasters should be required to make information from the political file available on the Internet rather than only through paper records at individual television stations. On April 27, 2012, the FCC approved new rules to require television broadcasters affiliated with the ABC, CBS, Fox, and NBC networks in the top 50 designated market areas (DMAs) to post political file information on the commission's website.[49] These rules took effect on August 2, 2012. Stations outside the top 50 DMAs or unaffiliated with the top four networks must comply as of July 2014.[50]

The implications of the new rules remain to be seen. The rules do not require that new information be made public, but the requirement to place ad-contract data online is a change in the status quo. The new requirements could enhance transparency by making "ad buy" data more quickly available and easily accessible. Drawing broad conclusions from the data, however, could be challenging. Broadcasters are required to post their political file information online, not to aggregate total costs or otherwise summarize advertising purchases in ways typically used by researchers and policy makers. It also appears that no standard file format is required.[51]

What Has Not Changed

Federal Ban on Corporate and Union Treasury Contributions

Corporations and unions are still banned from making contributions in federal elections.[52] PACs affiliated with, but legally separate from, those corporations and unions may continue to contribute to candidates, parties, and other PACs. As noted elsewhere in this report, corporations and unions may now use their treasury funds to make electioneering communications, independent expenditures, or both, but this spending is not considered a *contribution* under FECA.[53]

---

[48] The relevant provision appears in §504 of BCRA (P.L. 107-155). Although BCRA primarily amended FECA (2 U.S.C. §431 *et seq.*), the "political file" requirement amended the 1934 Communications Act. See 47 U.S.C. §315.

[49] Federal Communications Commission, *Second Report and Order*, In the Matter of Standardized and Enhanced Disclosure Requirements for Television Broadcast Licensee Public Interest Obligations, MM Docket No. 00-168, Washington, DC, April 27, 2012, http://transition.fcc.gov/Daily_Releases/Daily_Business/2012/db0427/FCC-12-44A1.pdf. See also Federal Communications Commission, "Standardized and Enhanced Disclosure Requirements for Television Broadcast Licensee Public Interest Obligations," 77 *Federal Register* 27631, May 11, 2012.

[50] See ibid and Federal Communications Commission, "Media Bureau Reminds Television Broadcasters of July 1, 2014 Online Political File Deadline," press release, April 4, 2014, http://transition.fcc.gov/Daily_Releases/Daily_Business/2014/db0404/DA-14-464A1.pdf.

[51] In addition to the rulemaking document cited above, see, for example, Justin Elliott, "FCC-Required Political Ad Data Disclosures Won't Be Searchable," *ProPublica* online, April 27, 2012, http://www.propublica.org/article/fcc-required-political-ad-data-disclosures-wont-be-searchable.

[52] 2 U.S.C. §441b.

[53] On the definition of *contribution*, see, in particular, 2 U.S.C. §431(8)(A) and 2 U.S.C. §441(b)(b)(2).

Federal Ban on Soft Money Contributions to Political Parties

The prohibition on using soft money in federal elections remains in effect. This includes prohibiting the pre-BCRA practice of large, generally unregulated contributions to national party committees for generic "party building" activities.

Some Contribution Limits Remain Intact

Pre-existing base limits on contributions to campaigns, parties, and PACs generally remain in effect. Post-*McCutcheon*, however, aggregate limits no longer apply. Therefore, although individuals are, for example, still prohibited from contributing more than $2,600 per candidate, per election during the 2014 cycle, the total amount of such giving is no longer capped. **Table 1** below and the table notes provide additional information, as do other CRS products.[54]

Despite *Citizens United's* implications for independent expenditures and electioneering communications, the ruling did not affect the prohibition on corporate and union treasury contributions in federal campaigns. As noted above, *SpeechNow* permitted unlimited contributions to independent-expenditure-only PACs (*super PACs*). The FEC has not issued rules regarding super PACs per se. In July 2011 the commission issued an advisory opinion stating that federal candidates (including officeholders) and party officials could solicit funds for super PACs, but that those solicitations were subject to the limits established in FECA and discussed below.[55] Also as noted elsewhere in this report, the FEC announced in October 2011, per an agreement reached in *Carey v. FEC*, nonconnected PACs would be permitted to raise unlimited amounts for independent expenditures if those funds are kept in a separate bank account.

In BCRA, Congress required that most contribution limits be biennially adjusted for inflation. However, Congress chose *not* to require adjustment of the PAC limits for inflation. Limits for the 2014 election cycle appear in **Table 1**.

---

[54] For additional discussion, see CRS Report R43334, *Campaign Contribution Limits: Selected Questions About McCutcheon and Policy Issues for Congress*, by R. Sam Garrett; CRS Report WSLG546, *Supreme Court To Hear Constitutional Challenge To Aggregate Contribution Limits*, by L. Paige Whitaker; and CRS Report WSLG363, *The Supreme Court, Citizens United, and Further Challenges to Campaign Finance Law: Aggregate Contribution Limits*, by L. Paige Whitaker.

[55] This matter was AO 2011-12 (Majority PAC and House Majority PAC). Majority PAC was formerly known as Commonsense Ten, noted above.

Table 1. Federal Contribution Limits, 2013-2014

(additional limits appear in the table notes)

Contributor	Recipient			
	Principal Campaign Committee	**Multicandidate Committee (most PACs, including leadership PACs)**	**National Party Committee (DSCC; NRCC, etc.)**	**State, District, Local Party Committee**
Individual	$2,600 per election*	$5,000 per year	$32,400 per year*	$10,000 per year (combined limit)
Principal Campaign Committee	$2,000 per election	$5,000 per year	Unlimited transfers to party committees	Unlimited transfers to party committees
Multicandidate Committee (most PACs, including leadership PACs)[a]	$5,000 per election	$5,000 per year	$15,000 per year	$5,000 per year (combined limit)
State, District, Local Party Committee	$5,000 per election (combined limit)	$5,000 per year (combined limit)	Unlimited transfers to party committees	Unlimited transfers to party committees
National Party Committee	$5,000 per election	$5,000 per year	Unlimited transfers to party committees	Unlimited transfers to party committees

Source: CRS adaptation from FEC, "Contribution Limits for 2013-2014," http://www.fec.gov/info/contriblimitschart1314.pdf.

Notes: The table assumes that leadership PACs would qualify for multicandidate status. The original source, noted above, includes additional information and addresses non-multicandidate PACs (which are relatively rare). Limits marked with an asterisk (*) are adjusted biennially for inflation. In addition to the invalidated limits noted in the table, *McCutcheon v. FEC* invalidated the following aggregate limits: (1) For individuals, a special biennial limit of $123,200 ($48,600 to all candidate committees and $74,600 to party and PAC committees) also applied. These amounts were adjusted biennially for inflation; (2) The national party committee and the national party Senate committee (e.g., the DNC and DSCC or RNC and NRSC) shared a combined per-campaign limit of $45,400, which is adjusted biennially for inflation.

a. *Multicandidate committees* are those that have been registered with the FEC (or, for Senate committees, the Secretary of the Senate) for at least six months; have received federal contributions from more than 50 people; and (except for state parties) have made contributions to at least five federal candidates. See 11 C.F.R. §100.5(e)(3). In practice, most PACs attain this status automatically over time.

Reporting Requirements

As noted above, developments resulting from the *Van Hollen* case and recent FCC rules require additional reporting surrounding EC donors and political advertising purchases (respectively). Nonetheless, disclosure requirements enacted in FECA and BCRA remain intact.[56] In general, political committees must regularly[57] file reports with the FEC[58] providing information about

- receipts and expenditures, particularly those exceeding an aggregate of $200;

- the identity of those making contributions of more than $200, or receiving more than $200, in campaign expenditures per election cycle; and

- the purpose of expenses.

Those making independent expenditures or electioneering communications, such as party committees and PACs, have additional reporting obligations. Among other requirements:

- Independent expenditures aggregating at least $10,000 must be reported to the FEC within 48 hours; 24-hour reports for independent expenditures of at least $1,000 must be made during periods immediately preceding elections.[59]

- The existing disclosure requirements concerning electioneering communications mandate 24-hour reporting of communications aggregating at least $10,000.[60] Donor information must be included for those who designated at least $200 toward the independent expenditure, or $1,000 for electioneering communications.[61]

- If 501(c) or 527[62] organizations make independent expenditures or electioneering communications, those activities would be reported to the FEC.[63]

---

[56] This excludes requirements that were subsequently invalidated, such as reporting associated with the now-defunct Millionaire's Amendment (which required additional reporting for self-funding above certain levels and for receipt of contributions in response to such funding). For additional discussion, see CRS Report RS22920, *Campaign Finance Law and the Constitutionality of the "Millionaire's Amendment": An Analysis of Davis v. Federal Election Commission*, by L. Paige Whitaker; and CRS Report RL34324, *Campaign Finance: Legislative Developments and Policy Issues in the 110th Congress*, by R. Sam Garrett.

[57] Reporting typically occurs quarterly. Pre- and post-election reports must also be filed. Non-candidate committees may also file monthly reports. See, for example, 2 U.S.C. §434 and the FEC's *Campaign Guide* series for additional discussion of reporting requirements.

[58] Unlike other political committees, Senate political committees (e.g., a Senator's principal campaign committee) file reports with the Secretary of the Senate, who transmits them to the FEC. See 2 U.S.C. §432(g).

[59] See, for example, 2 U.S.C. §434(g).

[60] 2 U.S.C. §434(f).

[61] Higher thresholds apply if the expenditures are made from a designated account. For additional summary information, see Table 1 in CRS Report R41264, *The DISCLOSE Act: Overview and Analysis*, by R. Sam Garrett, L. Paige Whitaker, and Erika K. Lunder. Donor information is reported in regularly filed financial reports rather than in independent expenditure reports.

[62] As the term is commonly used, *527* refers to groups registered with the Internal Revenue Service (IRS) as political organizations that seemingly intend to influence federal elections. By contrast, political committees (which include candidate committees, party committees, and political action committees) are regulated by the FEC and federal election law. There is a debate regarding which 527s are required to register with the FEC as political committees. For additional discussion, see CRS Report RS22895, *527 Groups and Campaign Activity: Analysis Under Campaign Finance and Tax Laws*, by L. Paige Whitaker and Erika K. Lunder.

[63] For additional discussion of these groups, see CRS Report RS21716, *Political Organizations Under Section 527 of* (continued...)

Potential Policy Considerations and Emerging Issues for Congress

Activity Thus Far During the 113th Congress

As shown in **Table 2** below, as of this writing, nine bills in the House and Senate have advanced beyond introduction during the 113th Congress. Two became law. H.R. 3487 reauthorized the FEC's Administrative Fine Program (AFP) until 2018. The bill also permits the commission to apply the program, which sets standard penalties for late campaign finance filings, to additional kinds of reports, such as those for independent expenditures. Another enacted bill, H.R. 2019, repealed public financing for presidential nominating conventions but does not affect appropriated security funding. The Senate Subcommittee on Crime and Terrorism held an April 9, 2013, hearing on enforcement of campaign finance law. On June 3, 2014, the Senate Judiciary Committee held a hearing on a proposed constitutional amendment (S.J.Res. 19) that, as introduced, would permit the states and Congress to regulate "money and in-kind equivalents with respect to Federal elections." On June 18, the Judiciary Committee's Subcommittee on the Constitution, Civil Rights and Human Rights marked up S.J.Res. 19. By a 5-4 rollcall vote, the subcommittee favorably reported the measure with subcommittee chairman Durbin's amendment in the nature of a substitute (ANS). Unlike the original bill, the ANS would permit Congress and the states to "regulate and set reasonable limits on the raising and spending of money by candidates and others to influence elections." As noted elsewhere in this report, the Senate also considered nominations to the FEC, and a Committee on House Administration hearing is scheduled on H.R. 186. That bill would permit candidates to designate someone other than the campaign treasurer to disburse campaign funds if the candidate died.

Table 2. Legislation Related to Campaign Finance that Has Advanced Beyond Introduction, 113th Congress

Bill Number	Short Title	Primary Sponsor	Brief Summary	Most Recent Major Action
H.R. 94	—	Rep. Cole	Would eliminate Presidential Election Campaign Fund (PECF) convention funding	Committee on House Administration markup held; bill ordered reported favorably 06/04/2013 (voice vote); reported 12/12/2013 (H.Rept. 113-291)

(...continued)

the Internal Revenue Code, by Erika K. Lunder; CRS Report R40183, *501(c)(4)s and Campaign Activity: Analysis Under Tax and Campaign Finance Laws*, by Erika K. Lunder and L. Paige Whitaker and CRS Report RS22895, *527 Groups and Campaign Activity: Analysis Under Campaign Finance and Tax Laws*, by L. Paige Whitaker and Erika K. Lunder.

Bill Number	Short Title	Primary Sponsor	Brief Summary	Most Recent Major Action
H.R. 95	—	Rep. Cole	Would eliminate PECF and transfer balance to the general fund of the U.S. Treasury for use in deficit reduction	Committee on House Administration markup held; bill ordered reported favorably 06/04/2013 (voice vote); reported 12/12/2013 (H.Rept. 113-292)
H.R. 1994	Election Assistance Commission Termination Act	Rep. Harper	Would eliminate Election Assistance Commission and assign specific National Voter Registration Act (NVRA) functions to the FEC	Committee on House Administration markup held; bill ordered reported favorably 06/04/2013 (voice vote); reported 12/12/2013 (H.Rept. 113-293)
H.R. 2019	Gabriella Miller Kids First Research Act	Rep. Harper	Relevant provisions of amended version of bill would eliminate PECF convention funding and convert amounts to "10-Year Pediatric Research Initiative Fund," with some amounts available to National Institutes of Health; contains health-research provisions unrelated to this report[a]	Became law 4/3/2014 (P.L. 113-94)
H.R. 2786; see also H.R. 3547	Financial Services and General Government Appropriations Act, 2014; see also FY2014 Consolidated Appropriations Act	Rep. Crenshaw	FY2014 Financial Services and General Government (FSGG) bill; Title V and §735 would prohibit reporting certain political contributions or expenditures as a condition of the government-contracting process	House Appropriations Committee reported as original measure (H.Rept. 113-172); placed on Union Calendar 07/23/2013; see also §735, H.R. 3547 (P.L. 113-76)

Bill Number	Short Title	Primary Sponsor	Brief Summary	Most Recent Major Action
H.R. 3487	—	Rep. Candice Miller	Extended until 2018 FEC authority to conduct the Administrative Fine Program, and expand program coverage to include additional reporting, such as non-candidate committees and independent expenditures	Became law 12/26/2013 (P.L. 113-72)
S. 375	Senate Campaign Disclosure Parity Act	Sen. Tester	Would require Senate political committees to file reports electronically and directly with the FEC	Senate Rules and Administration Committee markup held; reported favorably without written report 07/24/2013
S. 1371	Financial Services and General Government Appropriations Act, 2014	Sen. Tom Udall	FY2014 Financial Services and General Government (FSGG) bill; §621 would require Senate political committees to file reports electronically and directly with the FEC	Senate Appropriations Committee reported as original measure (S.Rept. 113-80); placed on Union Calendar 07/25/2013
S.J.Res. 19	—	Sen. Tom Udall	Proposed constitutional amendment that would permit Congress and the states to regulate "money and in-kind equivalents with respect to Federal elections"	Subcommittee on the Constitution, Civil Rights and Human Rights markup held, ordered favorably reported (5-4 vote) 06/18/2014; Senate Judiciary Committee hearing held 06/03/2014

Source: CRS analysis of bill texts.

Notes: The table excludes provisions in the Financial Services and General Government (FSGG) legislation regarding FEC appropriations and other provisions in the bill that might arguably be relevant, such as provisions concerning IRS training regarding political activities and requirements concerning reimbursement for political events hosted at the White House. Other measures tangentially related to campaign finance might also be relevant but are excluded from the table, which focuses on major provisions related to campaign finance issues.

a. For additional information on health-research provisions in the bill, congressional requesters may contact CRS Analyst Judith Johnson at x77077.

112th Congress

No major legislation primarily affecting campaign finance policy became law during the 112th Congress. The House passed two bills, H.R. 359 and H.R. 3463 (similar to H.R. 94 and H.R. 95 respectively in the 113th Congress), that would have repealed part or all of the presidential public financing program. Language in the 2012 Senate-passed farm bill (S. 3240) also would have repealed convention financing, but it was not included in the House version of the bill.[64] The House also passed H.R. 406, which would have permitted candidates to name someone other than the treasurer to disburse campaign funds if the candidate died. In addition, hearings were held on *Citizens United*; to oversee the FEC; on legislation to publicly finance congressional campaigns and to abolish the EAC and transfer some functions to the FEC; and on a draft executive order that might require additional disclosure of government contractors' political spending. Amendments adopted during consideration of unrelated bills (H.R. 1540, H.R. 2017, H.R. 2219, H.R. 2055, and H.R. 2354)[65] had implications for the contracting-disclosure debate. Two bills containing restrictions on contractor disclosure became law (H.R. 1540 and H.R. 2055).[66]

Emerging or Ongoing Policy Issues in Brief

Despite ongoing debate about whether or how to respond to *Citizens United*, there has been relatively little legislative momentum surrounding campaign finance since the 111th Congress (2010-2011). Various issues, nonetheless, remain prominent in Congress, the courts, at the FEC, or elsewhere in the policy community. This section briefly addresses those topics not discussed above but which appear to remain actively under consideration in Congress or at administrative agencies. Unless otherwise noted, this version of the report does not devote substantial attention to issues that appear not to be a major focus during the 113th Congress.

Disclosure to Agencies Other than the FEC

In addition to calls for regulation by the FEC, some lawmakers and interest groups have proposed that those making certain expenditures—particularly for political advertising—report to other agencies. Brief discussion appears below.

- Some Members of Congress have proposed providing additional information to shareholders if the companies in which they hold stock choose to make ECs or IEs.[67] Examples of legislation in the 113th Congress requiring shareholder notice of or approval for such expenditures include H.R. 1115, H.R. 1116 (Grayson), H.R. 1734 (Capuano), and S. 824 (Menendez). Other Members, however, oppose such proposals. As noted elsewhere in this report, appropriations measures have been used in previous Congresses to prohibit additional disclosures to the SEC.

---

[64] For additional discussion of convention financing, see CRS Report RL34630, *Federal Funding of Presidential Nominating Conventions: Overview and Policy Options*, by R. Sam Garrett and Shawn Reese. For additional discussion of the Senate-passed farm bill, see CRS Report R42552, *The 2012 Farm Bill: A Comparison of Senate-Passed S. 3240 and the House Agriculture Committee's H.R. 6083 with Current Law*, coordinated by Ralph M. Chite.

[65] See §§823, 713, 10015, 743, and 624 of the bills respectively.

[66] See §§823 and 743, respectively.

[67] For additional discussion, see CRS Report WSLG530, *Controversy about SEC's Being Asked to Require Disclosure of Political Donations*, by Michael V. Seitzinger.

Some "stand-alone" legislation also proposes to do so, such as H.R. 1626 (Wagner). In late 2013, the Securities and Exchange Commission (SEC) dropped plans to consider additional corporate disclosure of political spending.[68]

- In July 2010, citing *Citizens United*, the SEC issued new "pay-to-play" rules— which are otherwise beyond the scope of this report—to prohibit investment advisers from seeking business from municipalities if the adviser made political contributions to elected officials responsible for awarding contracts for advisory services.[69] The rules do not appear to have significantly affected federal campaign finance policy. It is possible, however, that they could have implications for local or state-level officials seeking federal offices from certain financial-sector fundraising.[70] During the spring of 2011, media reports indicated that the Obama Administration was considering a draft executive order to require additional disclosure of government contractors' political spending.[71] Implications of such an order would depend on final contents, if the order is issued. A draft of the order, however, generated attention in Congress and beyond. The House Committee on Oversight and Government Reform and Committee on Small Business held a joint hearing on the topic on May 12, 2011. As noted previously, provisions in an FY2014 appropriations bill, among other legislation, would prohibit such disclosure as a condition of the contracting process.

Revisiting Disclosure Requirements

Historically, disclosure aimed at reducing the threat of real or apparent conflicts of interest and corruption has received bipartisan support. In fact, disclosure typically has been regarded as one of the least controversial aspects of an otherwise often-contentious debate over the nation's campaign finance policy. Disclosure, then, could yield opportunities for cooperation among members of both major parties and across both chambers. On the other hand, some recent disclosure efforts have generated controversy. Particularly since the 111th Congress consideration of the DISCLOSE Act, some lawmakers raised concerns about whether the legislation applied fairly to various kinds of organizations (e.g., corporations versus unions) and how much information those airing independent messages rather than making direct candidate contributions should be required to report to the FEC. Revised versions of the legislation, introduced in the

---

[68] In 2012, the SEC's contribution to the Office of Information and Regulatory Affairs (OIRA) "Unified Agenda" (formally the *Unified Agenda of Regulatory and Deregulatory Actions*) indicated that the agency was considering developing a rule requiring disclosure of certain corporate political spending. The version of the Unified Agenda published in the fall of 2013 explained that the SEC was "withdrawing" the proposal but that future action was possible. On the Unified Agenda, see http://www.reginfo.gov/public/do/eAgendaMain. For brief additional discussion of the proposed rule, see, for example, Kenneth P. Doyle, "Disclosure of Corporate Political Spending Left Off SEC Agenda for New Regulations," *Daily Report for Executives*, December 3, 2013, p. A-1; and Dina ElBoghdady, "SEC Drops Disclosures of Corporate Political Spending from its Priority List," *The Washington Post*, December 1, 2013, p. A-8.

[69] See Securities and Exchange Commission, "Political Contributions by Certain Investment Advisers," 75 *Federal Register* 41018-41071, July 14, 2010.

[70] See, for example, Jake Bernstein, "How an Obscure Federal Rule Could Be Shaking Up Presidential Politics," *ProPublica*, August 28, 2012, http://www.propublica.org/article/how-an-obscure-federal-rule-could-be-shaking-up-presidential-politics.

[71] See, for example, Kenneth P. Doyle, "Anticipated Obama Order Would Require Disclosure of Contractors' Political Money," *Daily Report for Executives*, April 21, 2011, pp. A-6.

112th and 113th Congresses, do not contain spending restrictions, although some observers have questioned whether required reporting could inhibit spending.

Post-*Citizens United* legislative activity among those who favor additional disclosure has generally emphasized the DISCLOSE Act, but, as noted elsewhere in this report, some have also proposed reporting particular kinds of spending to agencies such as the IRS or the SEC. As 501(c) tax-exempt organizations' spending has received attention, measures proposing somewhat similar reporting as DISCLOSE, with additional tax implications (most of which are beyond the scope of this report) have also emerged. In the 113th Congress, one prominent example includes Senators Wyden and Murkowski's Follow the Money Act (S. 791). The bill has not been the subject of legislative action beyond introduction.[72]

Other key questions could be which type of disclosure should be required, if any, and of whom should that disclosure be required. Particularly for those organizations that do not typically have to report to the FEC (e.g., 527s or for-profit corporations), the House and Senate could require parity across all those receiving and spending funds affecting elections—even if those entities are not political committees or explicitly engaging in calls to elect or defeat candidates. Such an approach could be consistent with the historical emphasis on transparency in modern campaign finance policy, as noted throughout this report. Requiring additional reporting, however, could also raise questions about which entities should be regulated as political committees subject to federal election law—questions that have been controversial in the past.

Additional disclosure poses the advantage of making it easier to track the flow of political money. Disclosure, however, does not guarantee complete information, nor does it necessarily guard against all forms of potential corruption. For example, current requirements generally make it possible to identify which people or organizations were involved in a political transaction. This information promotes partial transparency, but does not, in and of itself, provide detailed information about what motivates those transactions or, in some cases, where the funds in question originated. Additional disclosure requirements from Congress, the FEC, or the IRS could provide additional clarity.

The Current Disclosure Process: How Reporting and Data Could Affect Policy Options and Considerations

Due in part to the disclosure requirements discussed above, some information about campaign fundraising and spending remains publicly unavailable. A variety of practical ramifications resulting from those requirements also affects availability of campaign finance information. If Congress chooses to revisit transparency in campaign funding and spending, attention to how these requirements operate in practice can shed light on which information is available, which is not, and why. The following selected ramifications, and others, of the current disclosure process could be relevant as Congress considers what policy problems exist and whether or how those problems should be addressed.

---

[72] For additional information, see *Comparison of Current Law with Selected Versions of the DISCLOSE Act and the Follow the Money Act*, August 20, 2013, by R. Sam Garrett, Erika Lunder, and L. Paige Whitaker; available to congressional requesters from the authors. The memorandum was prepared for distribution to multiple congressional offices.

- Unless meeting the criteria for disclosure,[73] corporate or union funds given to an intermediary (such as a trade association) for use in IEs or ECs do not have to be publicly reported. Accordingly, the total sources or amounts of corporate or union funds in federal elections remains unknown.

- Details about campaign spending are often unclear. For example, although campaign finance reports must contain itemized data providing general information about the nature of authorized committees' expenses greater than $200, political committees have wide latitude to characterize the expenses as long as the descriptions are not overly vague.[74]

- Political committees that file regular reports with the FEC do not have to provide information on spending in the final weeks of the campaign until 30 days after the general election. Some expenses might carry over to year-end reports. After reports are filed, additional time is required for the commission or outside researchers to adjust the data for amended filings and conduct analysis, particularly concerning individual transactions and fundraising and spending patterns. In some cases, "final" data are unavailable for several weeks or months. Paper filing of Senate reports, discussed elsewhere in this report, can also foster delay (although summary information is generally available within a few days).

- Recent initiatives to enhance the FEC website have made some campaign finance data far easier to access and analyze (especially for 2010 and later). However, accessing historical data can remain challenging. In particular, the FEC's Disclosure Data Catalog[75] provides easier access to data and more complete documentation than in the past. By contrast, much of the pre-2010 data have not yet been converted to the new formats and can require substantial time and technical expertise to access and interpret.

- Estimates (such as those appearing in some media accounts) that rely on partial data can be valuable and often provide more timely information than complete filings. However, estimates also require making assumptions that do not necessarily reflect technical distinctions in the data and among organizations. These differences may be unimportant for general summaries about which parties or groups raised or spent funds. More complete data, however, may be more likely to reflect important legal or regulatory distinctions among groups, account for amended filings, or address the details of particular transactions, including transfers among various organizations.

- Estimates sometimes report corporate and union activity differently. In particular, estimates about union spending might or might not report communications to members versus independent expenditures or electioneering communications. Similarly, estimates about corporate spending often include "corporations" as the

---

[73] For additional discussion, see CRS Report R40183, *501(c)(4)s and Campaign Activity: Analysis Under Tax and Campaign Finance Laws*, by Erika K. Lunder and L. Paige Whitaker.

[74] For example, listing the purpose of disbursement as "polling" is acceptable, but "outside services" is insufficient. See 11 C.F.R. §104.3(b)(3); 11 C.F.R. §104.3(b)(4). "Polling," in and of itself, however, does not explain the nature of the poll, whether the payee conducted the poll, analyzed the data, etc.

[75] The catalog is available at http://www.fec.gov/data/.

term is commonly understood, but do not necessarily include incorporated tax-exempt organizations or political committees.

- In general, fundraising and spending that is devoted only to issue advocacy is not publicly disclosed. As such, issue advocacy that arguably affects elections is often excluded from financial estimates. On the other hand, estimates that mix issue advocacy and express advocacy can inflate the amount of fundraising or spending that is truly dedicated to electoral politics.

- Currently, unlike all other federal political committees (except those raising or spending less than $50,000 annually), Senate campaign committees, party committees, and PACs are not required to file campaign finance reports electronically.[76] The lack of electronic filing leads to additional delay and cost in making complete Senate data publicly available. Electronic filing per se is generally non-controversial, although, in recent Congresses, there has been debate about whether "stand alone" electronic disclosure measures should be advanced or whether they should also address other issues.[77] Requiring electronic filing of Senate campaign finance reports might be an area of potential agreement in disclosure policy. The issue precedes *Citizens United* and other recent developments. As such, it is arguably a narrower policy concern, but also potentially a comparatively modest reform. As noted previously, during the 113th Congress, the Senate Committee on Rules and Administration held a markup on, and ordered favorably reported, S. 375, which would require Senate political committees to file their reports electronically and directly with the FEC rather than with the Secretary of the Senate, as is the current practice. The measure appears to have bipartisan support, but previous efforts to mandate electronic filing of Senate campaign finance reports have become embroiled in controversy surrounding unrelated amendments. Previously, some Senators also objected, as a matter of institutional prerogative, to changing the place of filing to the FEC.[78]

Each of the preceding points could be addressed as individual policy questions (e.g., through targeted legislation), but may also be a factor in any campaign finance proposal that would broadly affect disclosure policy. In either case, a potential policy question for Congress is whether the implications of the current reporting requirements represent "loopholes" that should be closed or whether existing requirements are sufficient. If additional information is desired, Congress, the FEC, IRS, or all three could revisit campaign finance law or regulation to require greater clarity about financial transactions that affect campaigns. As with disclosure generally, the decision to revisit specific reporting requirements will likely be affected by how much detail is deemed necessary to prevent corruption or accomplish other goals.

Revisiting Contribution Limits

After *Citizens United*, one potential concern is how candidates will be able to field competitive campaigns amid potentially unlimited corporate or union expenditures. One option for providing

---

[76] 11 C.F.R. §104.18(a).

[77] See, for example, CRS Report R40091, *Campaign Finance: Potential Legislative and Policy Issues for the 111th Congress*, by R. Sam Garrett.

[78] For historical discussion of the most recent previous debate over electronic filing, from the 111th Congress, see CRS Report R40091, *Campaign Finance: Potential Legislative and Policy Issues for the 111th Congress*, by R. Sam Garrett.

additional financial resources to candidates, parties, or both, would be to raise or eliminate contribution limits. However, particularly if contribution limits were eliminated, corruption concerns that motivated FECA and BCRA could reemerge. Raising contribution limits does not appear to have been actively considered in Congress since BCRA. Another option, which Congress has occasionally considered in recent years, would be to raise or eliminate current limits on coordinated party expenditures.[79] Coordinated expenditures allow parties to buy goods or services on behalf of a campaign—in limited amounts—and to discuss those expenditures with the campaign.[80]

In a post-*Citizens United* and post-*McCutcheon* environment, additional party-coordinated expenditures could provide campaigns facing increased outside advertising with additional resources to respond. Permitting parties to provide additional coordinated expenditures may also strengthen parties as institutions by increasing their relevance for candidates and the electorate. A potential drawback of this approach is that some campaigns may feel compelled to adopt party strategies at odds with the campaign's wishes in order to receive the benefits of coordinated expenditures.[81] Those concerned with the influence of money in politics may object to any attempt to increase contribution limits or coordinated party expenditures, even if those limits were raised in an effort to respond to labor- or corporate-funded advertising. Additional funding in some form, however, may be attractive to those who feel that greater resources will be necessary to compete in the modern era, or perhaps to those who support increased contribution limits as a step toward campaign deregulation.

FEC Issues

Federal Election Commission (FEC) matters have been the subject of prominent media attention, and some legislative activity, during the 113th Congress. Three items appear to be particularly noteworthy, as discussed below.

- During the summer of 2013, the Senate considered two nominations to the commission. Both were confirmed by unanimous consent, en bloc with two unrelated nominations, on September 23, 2013.[82] Both commissioners were sworn in and assumed office in late October.[83] As shown in **Table 3**, Ann Ravel (D) replaced former Commissioner Bauerly, who resigned from the agency

---

[79] This option would not provide campaigns with additional funding per se, but it could ease the financial burden on campaigns for those purchases that parties make on the campaign's behalf.

[80] Coordinated party expenditures are subject to limits based on office sought, state, and voting-age population (VAP). Exact amounts are determined by formula and updated annually by the FEC. For additional discussion, see CRS Report RS22644, *Coordinated Party Expenditures in Federal Elections: An Overview*, by R. Sam Garrett and L. Paige Whitaker; and CRS Report R41054, *Campaign Finance Policy After Citizens United v. Federal Election Commission: Issues and Options for Congress*, by R. Sam Garrett.

[81] The long-running debate about relationships between parties and candidates is well documented. For a brief overview, see, for example, Marjorie Randon Hershey, *Party Politics in America*, 12th ed., pp. 65-83; and Paul S. Herrnson, *Congressional Elections: Campaigning at Home and in Washington*, 4th ed., pp. 86-128.

[82] Sen. Reid, "Unanimous Consent Request—Executive Calendar," remarks in the Senate, *Congressional Record*, daily edition, vol. 159 (September 23, 2013), p. S6673.; and Sen. Reid, "Executive Calendar," remarks in the Senate, *Congressional Record*, daily edition, vol. 159 (September 23, 2013), p. S6674. The Senate Committee on Rules and Administration had ordered the nominations favorably reported by voice vote on September 17, 2013.

[83] Federal Election Commission, "Two New FEC Commissioners Assume Office; Will Hold Open Meeting on October 31," press release, October 28, 2013, http://www.fec.gov/press/press2013/news_releases/20131028release.shtml.

---

effective February 1, 2013. Lee Goodman (R) replaced former Commissioner McGahn, whose resignation was effective September 20, 2013.

Table 3. Current Members of the Federal Election Commission

Commissioner	Term Expires/Expired	Date Confirmed	Party Affiliation
Lee E. Goodman	04/30/2015	09/23/2013	Republican
Caroline C. Hunter	04/30/2013 (remains in holdover status)	06/24/2008	Republican
Matthew S. Petersen	04/30/2011 (remains in holdover status)	06/24/2008	Republican
Ann M. Ravel	04/30/2017	09/23/2013	Democrat
Steven T. Walther	04/30/2009 (remains in holdover status)	06/24/2008	Independent
Ellen L. Weintraub	04/30/2007 (remains in holdover status)	03/12/2003	Democrat

Source: Legislative Information System nominations database. Legislative Information System nominations database. CRS added party affiliation based on the seating chart distributed at FEC meetings.

- During the 113th Congress, FEC enforcement and transparency issues have attracted attention in Congress and beyond. In the House, the Committee on House Administration has continued to request documents from the agency about its enforcement practices. Major attention to the matter appears to have begun in November 2011, when the Committee on House Administration, Subcommittee on Elections, held an FEC oversight hearing—the first in almost a decade. Negotiations between the committee and commission appear to have resulted in the ongoing effort to approve and publicly release a new FEC enforcement manual. During the summer of 2013, controversy developed concerning an Office of General Counsel (OGC) draft of the manual and proposed revisions to that draft from Republican commissioners. A major source of controversy appeared to be the extent to which OGC staff should be permitted to initiate investigations or share information with other agencies (particularly the Justice Department) without specific commission authorization. Although the manual was scheduled for consideration at FEC open meetings at least as early as June 2013, it was held over due to disagreements among commissioners about whether a vote should be held, and if so, when. At a September 12, 2013, open meeting, commissioners held a lengthy and sometimes acrimonious discussion about when the manual would be considered and whether a vote to approve a final document should be held while nominees were pending in the Senate. As of this writing, the issue remains unresolved. It is also unclear how new commissioners might affect the debate.

- The commission has issued ad hoc guidance and advisory opinions about *Citizens United* and related litigation, but has not yet issued new regulations (or repealed old ones). The commission held a hearing on a notice of proposed rules in March 2012, but it is unclear when or whether new rules will be issued. Doing so would require agreement from at least four of six commissioners, something that has been difficult for the current commission on some recent, high-profile issues.

Public Financing Issues

At the federal level, public financing is limited to presidential campaigns. Additional detail is available in other CRS products.[84] Some supporters of publicly financed elections have suggested that this option could be a response to *Citizens United* in various kinds of campaigns. Regardless of whether public financing is pursued as a *Citizens United* or *SpeechNow* response, the presidential public financing program is widely regarded as needing restructuring if the system is to remain viable.[85] Some argue that the program should be eliminated either partially or entirely.

As this section explains, recent public financing matters before Congress concern efforts to repeal or amend the presidential public financing program and those to create a congressional public financing program. On a related note, a 2011 Supreme Court decision (*McComish*) primarily affects state-level programs but may be relevant for considerations of federal public financing options. Of these three areas, the presidential public financing program has received the most congressional attention recently.

Attempts in the 113th Congress to repeal or restructure the presidential public financing program mirror similar efforts from other recent Congresses. As noted in **Table 2**, Congress recently enacted, and the President signed, legislation repealing federal funding for presidential nominating conventions.[86] The Committee on House Administration has also reported related measures favorably (H.R. 94; H.R. 95; H.R. 1994). During the 112th Congress, the House passed a bill (H.R. 359) to repeal the presidential public financing program. Almost a year later, on December 1, 2011, the House again passed legislation (H.R. 3463) to end the public financing program. The latter bill combined the approach first passed in H.R. 359 with proposals to terminate the Election Assistance Commission (EAC). In the Senate, an amendment (containing text from S. 3257; see also H.R. 5912) to the 2012 Senate-passed farm bill, S. 3240, would have eliminated the convention funding portion of the presidential public financing program.[87] House measure H.R. 5912 would have also done so, as would Senate bill S. 3312. Another House bill, H.R. 6448, proposed to modernize the public financing program, but also would have eliminated convention funding.

In addition to efforts to repeal part or all of the public financing program, some Members have introduced proposals to restructure the program in an effort to make it more attractive to candidates. In general, recent proposals to revise the program would include increasing the match rate for primary contributions from the current 100% to at least 400% of small contributions. These and similar proposals could provide substantially greater resources to publicly financed candidates. This approach assumes that sufficient funds would be available in the PECF to cover the additional match, and that candidates would be willing to participate. Recent debate has also focused on whether or how the public financing program should maximize small contributions (e.g., those of less than $200).

---

[84] See CRS Report RL34534, *Public Financing of Presidential Campaigns: Overview and Analysis*, by R. Sam Garrett; CRS Report R41604, *Proposals to Eliminate Public Financing of Presidential Campaigns*, by R. Sam Garrett; and CRS Report RL34630, *Federal Funding of Presidential Nominating Conventions: Overview and Policy Options*, by R. Sam Garrett and Shawn Reese. Ongoing litigation, which is beyond the scope of this report, has placed some aspects of state-level programs in question.

[85] For additional discussion of proposals to publicly finance congressional campaigns, see CRS Report RL33814, *Public Financing of Congressional Campaigns: Overview and Analysis*, by R. Sam Garrett.

[86] Appropriated security funding is unaffected.

[87] The Coburn conventions amendment, no. 2214, passed 95-4; roll call vote no. 162.

In the 113th Congress, Representative Price reintroduced his 112th Congress bill, H.R. 6448, as H.R. 270. H.R. 270 is one of three bills introduced in the 113th Congress that would expand public financing for federal candidates. In addition to reforming the presidential public financing program, the Price legislation also proposes a new program to publicly finance House campaigns. Three other 113th Congress bills, H.R. 268 (Sarbanes), H.R. 20 (Sarbanes, which appears intended to supersede H.R. 268), and H.R. 269 (Yarmuth), offer different proposals to publicly finance House campaigns, but do not substantially address presidential public financing.

Finally, as noted previously, in March 2011, the Supreme Court of the United States heard oral arguments in two consolidated cases (*Arizona Free Enterprise Club's Freedom Club PAC et al. v. Bennett* and *McComish v. Bennett*). In *McComish*, the Court held that Arizona's matching fund system was unconstitutional.[88] The opinion is most relevant for state public financing programs in Arizona and elsewhere.[89] The presidential public financing program, which uses matching funds but does not base their award on opponents' or outside groups' spending, was not an issue in *Bennett*. The opinion suggests that policy mechanisms that attempt to "level the playing field" (a historic goal in some public financing proposals) could be unfeasible. Although some recent congressional public financing proposals have included funding based on opponents' activities, the legislation pending in the 113th Congress (discussed above) would award matching funds—at the presidential and congressional levels—based only on the publicly financed candidate's fundraising.

IRS Notice of Proposed Rulemaking Concerning Certain 501(c) Entities

In November 2013, the Internal Revenue Service (IRS) and the Treasury Department announced a notice of proposed rulemaking (NPRM) that could significantly affect how some tax-exempt organizations engage in campaign activity. As of this writing, it appears that the proposed rules will be superseded by a new proposal to be released in the future. This section retains material on the November 2013 NPRM for historical reference and in case the material remains relevant. This section will be updated as additional information about the expected new IRS proposal becomes available.

The November 2013 NPRM focused on 501(c)(4) groups, although the document also solicited input about whether 501(c)(5) labor unions and 501(c)(6) trade associations should also be addressed. Other CRS products that focus on tax law provide additional detail, much of which is beyond the scope of this report.[90]

- The draft rules are potentially important for campaign finance policy because the NPRM borrows key terms from federal election law and because those favoring additional regulation of 501(c) entities generally call for a closer alliance between tax policy and law and campaign finance policy and law. Currently, because 501(c) organizations are not *political committees* as defined in FECA,

---

[88] 131 S.Ct. 2806 (2011).

[89] See CRS Report RL33814, *Public Financing of Congressional Campaigns: Overview and Analysis*, by R. Sam Garrett. This report does not attempt to determine *Bennett's* applicability in other states.

[90] See CRS Report R40183, *501(c)(4)s and Campaign Activity: Analysis Under Tax and Campaign Finance Laws*, by Erika K. Lunder and L. Paige Whitaker; CRS Report WSLG168, *501(c)(4)s and Campaign Activity: How Much Is Too Much?*, by Erika K. Lunder; and CRS Report WSLG519, *What Does the Law Say About 501(c)(4)s and Campaign Activity?*, by Erika K. Lunder.

they do not fall under FEC or FECA requirements unless they make ECs or IEs.[91] Nonetheless, many such groups engage in activity that might influence campaigns. In recent years, debate has developed about whether such activity should be subject to additional regulation.

- In its NPRM, the IRS proposes a new concept, "candidate-related political activity," to replace its current facts-and-circumstances-based determination of a group's primary purpose. Under the draft rules, various election-related activities—such as advocating the election or defeat of candidates during pre-election periods, get-out-the-vote (GOTV) activities, or preparing voter guides— would not qualify as promoting social welfare, which is supposed to be 501(c)(4) groups' primary purpose. The draft rules do not specify "how much" candidate-related political activity would be permitted. It is unclear precisely what form final rules will take or when they might be issued.

- In April 2014, IRS Commissioner John Koskinen stated in prepared remarks that the agency had received more than 150,000 comments on the proposed rules, that the agency might revise the draft guidance in response to those comments, and that the rulemaking was unlikely to be completed by the end of 2014.[92]

- On June 18, 2014, the Center for Public Integrity reported that, in an interview with the organization, Commissioner Koskinen said that the IRS "will propose new and specific rules defining how much money 'social welfare' nonprofits may spend on political campaigns." The new proposal is expected "by early 2015."[93]

Authority to Disburse Campaign Funds

The Committee on House Administration has announced a June 25, 2014, hearing to consider H.R. 186 (Jones). The bill would permit candidates to designate to the FEC an individual to direct campaign spending following the candidate's death. That designation would supersede the campaign treasurer's normal spending responsibilities, but would not affect the treasurer's reporting responsibilities. A backup could also be identified if the designee died, became incapacitated, or were unable or unwilling to carry out his or her responsibilities. The bill also permits candidates to specify their wishes about how funds would be disbursed.

The House has passed three substantially similar measures, also sponsored by Representative Jones, in recent Congresses. As noted previously, this included H.R. 406, which passed the House in September 2012. In addition, on April 22, 2009, H.R. 749 passed the House by voice vote and under suspension of the rules. H.R. 749 was virtually identical to H.R. 3032, which the House passed on July 15, 2008, also under suspension of the rules and by voice vote. The House passed

---

[91] If the groups had an affiliated super PACs, the super PAC would report to the FEC as a political committee.

[92] John Koskinen, Commissioner, Internal Revenue Service, *Prepared Remarks of Commissioner of Internal Revenue Service John Koskinen before the National Press Club*, Internal Revenue Service, IR-2014-42, Washington, DC, April 2, 2014, http://www.irs.gov/uac/Newsroom/Prepared-Remarks-of-Commissioner-of-Internal-Revenue-Service-John-Koskinen-before-the-National-Press-Club. See also, for example, Josh Hicks, "IRS Firm on Exemption Reforms," *Washington Post*, April 17, 2014, p. A13.

[93] Julie Patel, "IRS Chief Promises Stricter Rules for 'Dark Money' Nonprofit Groups," Center for Public Integrity, June 18, 2014, http://www.publicintegrity.org/2014/06/18/14960/irs-chief-promises-stricter-rules-dark-money-nonprofit-groups.

all three bills with bipartisan support and minimal debate. The Senate took no action on any of these bills.

As Congress considers H.R. 186, it may be useful to consider how FECA currently addresses campaign-spending authority. FECA assigns campaign treasurers primary responsibility for filing FEC reports and ensuring that political committees comply with the act.[94] Treasurers—not candidates—are legally responsible for disbursing campaign funds.[95] In fact, FECA does not specify a role for candidates in campaign financial decisions. Of course, as a practical matter, however, candidates may exert substantial informal influence over campaign spending.

The proposal contained in H.R. 186 and its predecessors could alleviate the potential for asset disputes following candidate deaths—a topic about which some Members have raised concern. That outcome, however, depends on designees adhering to candidate wishes, and assumes that designees would be more faithful to candidate wishes than would be treasurers.

Because FECA is currently silent on candidate-spending authority, H.R. 186 could create different levels of candidate authority over spending in life than in death. Although H.R. 186 would provide a mechanism for circumventing the treasurer after a candidate dies, the bill would not provide additional remedies for such action while the candidate is living. This may be a minor distinction due to candidates' *de facto* influence over their campaigns, despite FECA's general silence on the issue. Nonetheless, if Congress chose to enact the bill and felt it were important to create parity in candidates' abilities to direct campaign spending, it could amend FECA to create a clearer candidate role over campaign funds regardless of whether the candidate is living or dead. Congress might also provide explicit permission in FECA for candidates to hire and fire campaign treasurers.

Conclusion

Some elements of federal campaign finance policy have substantially changed in recent years; others have remained unchanged. Enactment of BCRA in 2002 marked the culmination of efforts to limit soft money in federal elections and place additional regulations on political advertising airing before elections. BCRA was an extension of efforts begun in the 1970s, with enactment of FECA, to regulate and document the flow of money in federal elections. BCRA's soft-money ban and some other provisions remain in effect; but *Citizens United*, *SpeechNow*, and other litigation since BCRA have reversed major elements of modern campaign finance law. In particular, corporate and union spending that is now permissible has not previously been allowed in modern elections.

The changes discussed in this report suggest that the nation's campaign finance policy may be a continuing issue for Congress. Disclosure requirements, a hallmark of federal campaign finance policy, remain unchanged. Additional information would be required to fully document the sources and rationales behind all political expenditures. For some, such disclosure would improve

---

[94] See, for example, 2 U.S.C. §432(a). On treasurer responsibilities, see 2 U.S.C. §434(a)(1); 2 U.S.C. §432(c); and 2 U.S.C. §432(d).

[95] See, for example, 11 C.F.R. §102.7(c). Other designees, such as assistant treasurers, may also perform treasurer duties. See also Federal Election Commission, *Committee Treasurers*, brochure, Washington, DC, March 2007, http://www.fec.gov/pages/brochures/treas.shtml.

transparency and discourage corruption. For others, additional disclosure might be viewed with suspicion and as a potential sign of government intrusion. Particularly in recent years, tension has also developed between competing perspectives about whether disclosure limits potential corruption or stigmatizes those who might choose to support unpopular candidates or groups. Fundraising, spending, and reporting questions have been at the forefront of recent debates in campaign finance policy, but they are not the only issues that may warrant attention. Even if no legislative changes are made, additional regulation and litigation are likely, as is the constant debate over the role of money in politics. Although some of the specifics are new, these themes discussed throughout this report have been present in campaign finance policy for decades.

Author Contact Information

R. Sam Garrett
Specialist in American National Government
rgarrett@crs.loc.gov, 7-6443